Mela

Dick Sullivan

Coracle Books

By the same author:
Prose: *Navvyman*
   Old Ships, Boats and Maritime
    Museums
Verse: *Capperbar*
   Morning on the Mountain
   The Moon at Midnight

The Odyssey in Brief was first published
in *Aesthetica Magazine*, March 2005

ISBN 0 9062 80 33 8

Published by Coracle Books
13 Red House Yard
Thornham Magna
Eye
Suffolk IP23 8HH

Capperbar@hotmail.com

For Mary

Contents

Part Two

Preface 1

Dear Melanie,

"What is love?" you asked today, and I had no ready reply.

Another summer evening ends in rain and the plane trees in the alleyway are dark green and fading into dusk. These are my thoughts for you:

Only thought can be shown to exist and when thought is stilled, love flows in.

But what if we could prove that matter also does exist? Well, above it, and issuing from it, is immaterial thought which, when stilled, is love.

Love, then, is the only thing we can know, the only thing we can be sure exists. Love is the maker and we are made out of it.

Love comes in many shapes but the most important is that between a man and a woman. Human love is Love Itself writ small.

This smaller love is a dilute form of the Greater and so is a spiritual experience in its own right.

For some, love is what gives life point, purpose and meaning. It is a sure way to peace and happiness and a sense that life is precious and necessary and worth the pain that comes willy-nilly with it. Without it we merely exist, endure, get by, accept, make do, trudge on, and wait to die. To Love Itself, this be must sin. Were we given life to throw it so wantonly away?

People marry for many reasons, you say. Well, yes, but perhaps for the wrong ones. Or love comes to us so late, that terrible mistakes have already been made. To deny it when it comes, however, is wrong and destructive. In my view love not only comes from God but is God in a pale and filtered down kind of way.

Love ends the isolation of the self, of selfishness, and aloneness since you now live for another. We are designed to belong to an entity greater than ourselves and, for some, love is the only way of achieving it.

When you love you see the worth of another human in the way God sees it: all faults forgivable and forgiven. It is to feel joy and happiness in her presence. It is to want to care, protect, cherish, serve and save. It is to want nothing but her good and her happiness and to want nothing for yourself except to be with her and be allowed to love.

Physical love is its highest expression. Base sex with another then becomes wrong, a betrayal and a denial of love. Only love sanctifies the physical and it in turn gives us our deepest insight into the fullness at the heart of things.

"Few things matter very much," said Stanley Baldwin, our one time Prime Minister, "and most things don't matter at all." But love matters, and in the end is the only thing that does. Without it, we are nothing: with it, we are close to God."Who loveth not, knoweth not God, for God is love."

Love, R
London, August 2005

Preface II

Dear Melanie,

What is poetry? (I ask). What is its point or purpose? My reply is unorthodox, unfashionable, anti-zeitgeist but not, I think, wrong (or at least not too wrong).

To begin at the bottom, poetry in English is a pattern of stressed and unstressed syllables.

It's rare (verse is common) and memorable, sliding easily into the mind and memory and staying there.

It delights, brings joy, and enlarges the mind and consciousness, making us into better people.

It works by shocking the thinking mind into stillness. Into this void flows the deepest thing we can know: Love, the Creator.

It seems to work in two ways; through an image conveyed by words, and through the sound of syllables in combination, rather like music, perhaps.

To some poets, like Swinburne, sound is all. Provence, to him, was less a place, more a euphony:

By a tideless dolorous midland sea
In a land of sand and ruin and gold.

Images alone can shut down the mind, too. Prose translations of Japanese haiku work on this level: "a view of the sea through summertime pines and a temple lantern cut from stone."

Poetry is spiritual. Through it we briefly meet God, of whom we are in any case made.

A big claim, yes? Well, yes, but that's my vision. Poetry is the flow of the timeless through time back into timelessness. It merely passes through us, changing us as it goes.

The centre of our city is calm and empty on a hot Sunday afternoon in summer. The sidewalks are all mine; I choose the shade. Without you, all the poetry in the world is nothing but an emptiness.

Love, R
London, August 2005

Preface III

Dear Melanie,

Capperbar is not easy to follow, you say? Would a few notes help – if it's worth deciphering at all, that is?

It began with the question: "can faith and empiricism be reconciled?"

Empiricism, of course, is the English philosophy of doubt underpinning the Enlightenment. All we can know, it tell us, comes to us through our senses – sight, taste, touch, hearing. It follows, therefore, that what is above nature, the super-natural, is unknowable.

But it can't deny what is experienced and *Capperbar* is about the experience of something greater than the self, a deepness that transforms and changes you. It happens when the thinking mind is shut down and its endless restlessness stilled. It is then that we meet Greaterness, and the certainty that we see into the very heart of things.

This experience, in fact, is the end-point of philosophy-religions such as Taoism and Zen. Zen calls it *satori*, or enlightenment, and has perfected its own techniques for inducing it. All involve closing down thought to let Deeperness and Greaterness take over.

Plato knew it, too. To him, it was the real reality beyond the reach of the senses, perfection in the changeless realm of Being. Its highest point he called The Good though in time he came to see it as God and, later still, as Love

A philosopher, according to Plato, is anybody who's been touched by this ultimate reality and been transformed by it. The effects of this experience are empirically testable, presumably, in changes in the brain. They're of great value, whatever they are.

But Capperbar has a second theme as well; the study of the inward- dwelling temperament, and that inner space (big as the cosmos) where it feels most at home and where Greaterness is most readily met.

The word capperbar is Nelsonic sea-slang for anything looted or stolen and here is also the name of the protagonist in a short narrative poem. Capperbar, the man, has been stolen by the Press Gang and forced into an alien world. It is, in a way, an allegory of this life: we don't ask to be here, and many find it unbearable. What is experienced by the stilled mind is the only consolation open to him at his death. It isn't enough.

Capperbar, too, is a poetry of place, since landscape is one way of inducing our sense of Greaterness.

Let's go briefly through it:

We open with Royal Navy officers drinking a toast (in blackstrap wine) to Lord St Vincent's victory over the French on St Valentine's Day, 1797. Men like these are unafraid: Capperbar is fear itself.

This leads to the second main theme: the inner-looking nature, what it is, and what it is like to live there.

Next, we follow the narrator's lifelong search for meaning, point and purpose: each episode ends in failure.

Brundisium stands for friendship, after the poem by Horace in which he tells of a journey across the marshes and over the mountains to Brindisi with Virgil on the Emperor's diplomatic business. Horace, of course, was famous for his friendships.

In Part Two, the narrator meets the deepest thing we can know in the cavern of the mind where, at moments of stillness, he talks to God.

His first experience of Greaterness, as a four year old child in wartime Westmorland, was triggered by briars against the Spring sky. To the child, still fumbling with language, the brambles were trees, not bushes Ever after, the brambletree was his own private symbol for what induced Greaterness, and what was induced by it.

All his life this vision has been his and he sees it again in an all-steel 20th century London coffee shop. The vision comes unbidden, as it always has, and elevates and elates, as it always does.

In *Godfound*, we look at other things which induce the Divine; music (ebony and air), art, carp in a pond, sunshine and shade, rain stains on a brick. This is the bramblesight that sees the fullness at the heart of things.

We then move to the poet's final experience of decay and death. This leads him to realise there is a deeper truth than he has so far uncovered, that he's only ever been half right, if never wholly wrong. That truth is the theme of this book's sequels: *Morning on the Mountain*, *The Moon at Midnight* and *Melanie*.

Yet he's still a child of the Enlightenment (he never abandons it, or decries the philosophy underlying it) and he goes on to question the validity of religion, and puts up a few second hand ideas about how the hereafter can be reconciled with science.

Addendum is a collection of poems illustrating most of the above points: more particularly, perhaps, the power of landscape to induce Greaterness. *Quakerman* looks at that bit of

Christianity closest to the poet's own very private insight, the Inner Light of Fox. *Paintings, RA* is about an exhibition of Scottish Colourists in the Royal Academy, now many years ago and forgotten.

Love, R
London, August 2005

Preface IV

Monologue

No, the inward-dwelling mind is not easy to talk about, is it? Is that why nobody does? People shy away. Why? Well, people do, don't they, when they don't understand? Is it too unknown to too many people?

On the fells above the navvy village in Mardale there's a "cave": in fact, it's an old adit mine abandoned when the copper lode ran out. It's only a few yards deep and never wholly dark, though it plips and plops nicely with water.

In the North York Moors and in the Mendips are real caves: miles of passageways, and caverns and rivers and lake and stalactites, all lightless and blind. A counter-country, in fact, made by rain in limestone hills.

Perhaps most people's inner cave is like the Mardale copper mine: mine is like the Mendips.

There are two worlds, therefore: an inside one and an outside, an inner and an outer.

Inside is where it all happens. When thought is still, you leave time and enter here. It is a counter-cosmos entered through the mind, but more real than the diurnal planet of sea and stone. It is not just where love lives, it is Love. Where the matterless speaks to matter. What words can I make up to describe this place which is not a place but is all-place because it is ultimately all there is. (Or at least that's how it feels. I make no claim to infallibility.)

Does nobody else see it? You out there! Is this so unknowable to you? This is a fellow-human speaking yet I am unable to reach you or interest your mind. Is common humanity not enough to convince you you should listen?

Signals cross space and enter time to where you are but you seem to lack an aerial to pick them up.

I have no hands, no atoms, with which to touch you. Is it like a two-way mirror? I see you, you see only yourself?

Mutual misunderstanding is here. We don't know each other. How quickly you take offence. Why? Ego or I, I suppose. In here there is no I or ego. Do you think you'll live forever?

And yet it not enough. Without human love, it is not enough; we are more matter than we are the matterless, more flesh than spirit.

London, October 2005

Part One

Prologue:

Melanie in the Street

"She walks towards me in the street,
How small she is, and neat,
How compactly made, how rare,
How perfect on her feet."

"Her face is framed by hair
And she smiles that I am there,
That I am there to greet her
As I too stop to stare."

"A private little smile, and shy,
She dips her head and I know why
I love her so and care
And why to see her is to melt and die."

"Down she looks to smile,
So womanly all the while,
She is my home where I can rest
As she puts her mouth to mine."

"As we embrace I feel her breast
So loving on my chest
And with my hand I touch her face
And am in turn caressed."

"This is a poor and dingy place
But I feel that we are touched by grace,
And as we walk together hand in hand
Of dinginess there is no trace."

A Gentle Man

Only a gentle man can give
All the love I need to live.

Tears come quickly to your eye
(How easily I make you cry)

Yet you comfort me as only you can
With the strength and the love of a gentle man

For I need that gentle man's caress
To ease my pain, and my distress.

Alone you sees me as truly I am
For I am only truly myself with my gentle man.

Oh, my most tender, most gentle of men,
Please love me forever, as only you can.

Love-in-Age I

Are you, I ask him, still my friend?
"Yes," he tells me simply,
"Till the love of God shall end."

Your love for me won't falter
But always will increase?
"Yes," he tells me gently,
"Till the love of God shall cease."

When I'm too old for loving
Will you love me still?
"When God no longer loves you,
I most surely will"

Love in Age II

In your arms no sadness is;
You are the sweetness of my life,
My balm. You will never tire
Of me? Never wish me gone?

"Not till the setting of my final sun
For I am passed my changing time."

Love in Age III

In gentleness you envelop me,
A gentleness of touch and of caress,
A gentleness of mind.
Tell me you will never change.

"I have reached my final stage;
I am the constancy of love
And the quietness of age
And am tempered too by time."

Love in Age IV

You see the splinters in my soul,
You see the shards that lacerate
And the brokenness bequeathed by fate.
Are you here to heal me and to mend?

"I need to heal the hurt in you
Or I too am wounded unto death.
For you are my destination, and my end."

Gift

What gift, l ask you, can I give?
"Your inner hurt," you gently say,
"And let me be your remedy."

"I beg you, please,
To trust me with your soul
And let me give you ease
And let me make you whole."

But helpless you stand
And stroke my face
And oh, so gently stroke my hand.

So Much

And all the things that time has taught
Have never taught me love like this;

Never have I known such love,
Never knew such love could be;

Never knew someone could love me so
Or make such love to me

For passion too had passed me by
But passion too has come unsought

And when together on our bed we lie
I know that Love itself can never die

For I know I'm in the arms of Love.
And Love has taught me, oh, so much.

The Green of Summer

What you say I know is true:
There is a depth of love
Between us two for we share
A common root.

Neither of us can live alone
Though alone we've always had to live.
What greater gift has God to give?

You are my summertime where I am
Safe and warm and where no winter is,
No Autumn storm. Let me live
Forever in the green of your summer
For I have seen in you my own true home.

Sharing

I've not been taught to share
But now I want to share with you
If you can teach me how.

To share it seems I must
Give way to love, and trust
The man I love to love me too;
And that, my darling, I shall do.

When the wound in me begins to heal
Then I no longer shall conceal
The love I feel for you.

Skirt

Blue is not my colour,
I always thought,
And yet we bought
This skirt some weeks ago
And today I wear it as we go
To the little hills which are
Nearly now our own.

Am I too old
For something so
In fashion? Is it too
Flamenco-like for me?

"Underneath your pain and hurt
You are art and love and passion,
Not the passion of these pale hills
But of fierce and sharp sierras.
You are stamping shoes and castanets,
A life that's lived without regrets
For you are elemental in the sun."

"Elemental is what you are
Dancing to a wild guitar"

"And a gipsy skirt can still express
That lady, undamaged by distress,
Who still is there beneath a hurt
And broken heart."

Chiltern

What a perfect and a simple day:
Tea and scones and you and I alone
Above an unseen river in a hollow
In green and timbered hills.

Tell me what the future now will bring?
When the nettle's dead it still can sting.

"I am your quietness,
The place where you belong.
We are love, and love can do no wrong."

Long Ago

Tell me of the summertime
In your boyhood long ago;
Tell me, for you are mine
And I most surely need to know.

Oh, tell me of the gentle counties
In your boyhood long ago.
Heal me with your gentleness
And tell me that you love me so.

"I have no yesterday
For you weren't there:
You are the object of my quest,
I find you and still I find no rest."

Today

Where were you today, my little boy,
So lost and lonely on your own?

"Where the willows are, like long-
Haired heads neck deep in earth,
And by the waterway."

But I too was lost and all alone,
In company .

Absence

Today I couldn't phone.
Did you miss me? Miss my call?

"In pain I cried,
Pacing paving stones,
Without you by my side."

I hunger for you too. Both
of us so lost and so alone.

"Your reflection now is missing
From the mirror in the hall."

I miss you so
And feel so lonely and so low;

This pain is ours. I share it too,
For I also give my love to you.

My Thoughts

I know you grieve
For want of me. But you too
Never leave my mind
And my thoughts are all of you.
I never knew that love
Could be so deep
So tender and so true.

Away 1

"You've set me such a task
While you're away; 'Can
We be merely friends
Again,' you ask."

"I do not have to think;
I merely have to draw my breath
To know the answer
Is my death if you insist
The answer's yes."

The sun is beating on the bay
Making smooth a glinting sea
And what you say I know is truth.

Away II

Here in the south the sun is high
Blazing on a hillside, burnt and dry.

Does our city now before you lie,
Now you are free to walk? Only with you
Do I feel free and safe and safe at home
But I walk beside an alien sea.

"I'm free to walk, but free
Of you I can never be.
A husk of body walks the street
But I am with you on that beach."

Away III

"Today I walked by the riverside
Before the turning of the tide
And the stream flowed backwards from the sea."

"Everywhere your question came with me
(Can we again be merely friends?).
Undistracted, I near despair."

"I stand within the painted O
And note not one of the spells
Of Prospero can order love."

"Throw away thy magic book
Is what this tale tells me
And put thy faith in greater things:
We two are hooped by golden rings."

Away IV

Please be true to me while I'm away
Though I'm not free to live with you
I cannot share, and need you for my own.

"I've painted all the walls of all the rooms
And, on the balcony you still call mine
(Though all I have is yours),
I've dug in flowers in bloom in pots for you."

"Now a cheddar-yellow moon
Is held in air behind the alley trees
And throws quick shadows
On a pale magnolia wall,
To lift and flicker, fade and fall."

"This great city spins in sex and sin
But I am true. I am here for you alone
And if you need me for your own
Then I am yours."

I watch the self-same moon above the sea
And long for you, and home, for home
To me is you. Be true to me.

Away V

"Can we again be simple friends, you'll ask
On your return (and soon, near the end
Of hot sharp-shadowed June.)"

"The dome of Paul's upon its drum
Tells of death, and the life to come"

"But Paul, that odd old man,
So small and flawed, taught us all
That all there is is love."

"So amid the gilding and the gold
All I want is you to hold"

"For I need the love that walks
Abroad on human feet,
Like my shy lady in the street."

"All that glitter, all that gold:
There is no guilt in love."

I've been unfair to you: it seemed
So wrong to tell you of my love
When I'm not free.

I'd not been taught to share,
And couldn't share my love
With you who share your love
With me.

Yet this year I've grown to know
You all my life. You are my husband,
I your unwed wife.

"Can we again be friends? you ask.
The answer's always now the same."

"The chequered floor of Paul's
Is starkly black and white and easy,
A chess board for a subtle game."

"High in the lantern is a haze of light;
But who is king and who the knight?
And if we defy God's love where will we end?"

"Days will shorten, dark increase,
And we shall know that life must cease
And see the ruin that's to come
And we shall wonder what we missed.
Shall we sit and write the list?"

"This is a love that came unsought.
Each of us alone is naught,
We need two to make a one.
And life will soon enough be done."

Away VIII

Today I bought a paper
In a paper shop
And wondered if this age
Is really ours. All that sex
On shelves is a mockery
Of love.

Today I was rebuked also
For writing God is love.
"It's stale," a lady scolded me:
But no, not so. It is truth,
The only truth that we can know.

And it's through the love between us two
That we both know that it is true.
We meet God when we make love.
So, no, we can't again be merely friends.

At Peace

I phone and you are there. You
Always are. Today I called
And again you came. You
Always do. All we did was drive
To where I did my chore.
Then back we drove
Through London traffic, brash
And noisy. "Are you at peace?"
You asked. What a lovely way
You talk! "Yes," I said,
"You sit beside me and I am."
And the traffic ground and grated
All around and I was there, with you,
At peace.

Gift I

"Once last summer we used to meet
In the painted church in Margaret Street
With its saffron saints and organ pipes
In gold and blue. And I watched their deep"

"Effect on you. I'd seen a thousand
Shuffling feet, shod in trainer shoes,
That barely paused before retreating
Out of doors. But you, you were transfixed,"

"Enraptured in the aisle
Where manger
And the magi meet on tile;
Then straightaway I knew
There is the gift of art in you."

Gift II

"The opposite of change
Is never rest. It is decay."

"What you are, that must you be
As the acorn grows to the great oak tree."

"And you are deep and have
A gift that is not yours
To shun or disobey;"

"It is not yours to gather or to get.
It is given and you should let
The art-gift grow in you;"

"Then you must repay the Giver
By giving back the gift to all."

Gift III

"Is it wrong for me to tell
You what to do? But plead or tell,
We hear the tolling of a passing bell."

"What will we be
If we fail to act or do?
Time is not eternity
And the glitter of the morning dew
Is far too far away for us to see."

Gift IV

"I read you verse in the car today
And right away you saw its fault."

"This afternoon to ease you
In the doctor's waiting room
I pointed to a painting of a vase
And flowers in summer bloom
And straightaway you saw its flaw."

"It lacks a yellow and a red
To lift the picture, which is dead,
Intuitively you said."

"Art is to enlarge and let
Those around you grow.
Do not let a good gift go,
Disused and wasted."

Gift V

I cannot do what I want to do
Which is to live alone with you.

"But you believe, and God
Has made you what you are
And your desires are therefore
Right and true."

"And He has told you what to do:
Follow the love he gave to you
And the gift of understanding art."

Dismissal

"Again you send me right away
While you're unhappy and in pain."

"I shelter in a teashop from the rain
And sit and think and wrack my brain
How can I help. In vain."

"For I am powerless. I cannot act.
Yours is the power. The will alone you lack."

I am so full of fear. Can you not see?
But I'll always need your love for me.

"On you the burden is too great
Yet what can I do but sit, and wait?"

The Cool of the Morning Sun

"Today we saw the Columbia Hills
All cut from gold and gleaming
In a picture sent from Mars"

"And a frozen lake of water blue
As southern seas in a crater
Ochred by our own bright sun."

"And you marvelled
At the yellow sky above
The ice-made hills of Titan,
Cut by methane rain and rivers
Flowing to a methane sea."

"Here, another summer evening dies
In damp. The wireless plays.
And we can never go
To where the salt sea waters break
And light is born upon the deep
Of our own deep ocean-seas."

No. But how I long to go,
To breakfast on a balcony
In the cool of the morning sun
And be alone with you
The whole day long.

Equinox

"Another Equinox, and war
In arid places where young men
Go to die. We live
In love when in our arms we lie."

Untitled

"There is no guile in you
Yet guilelessly you pretend
That all is well to fool
A foolish world
And succeed."

You know me better than
I know myself. Will you always
Be my guide to me?

Naivety

Tell me truly, am I naïve? Is
That something you believe?

"Innocence without pretence?
Open, candid, lacking guile?
Artless, uncunning and unsly?"

"If you are naïve,
Then I believe naïve is best.
Please be forever simple.
Be unlike the rest."

"In you there is nothing that's unkind,
No crooked timber of mankind."

Midnight

Midnight is my hour and time
To hear the cracked bronze bell
Of Pancras chime
In the hollow of the vale.
Midnight is my hour and mood
And as the heat of day grows chill,
I have the night ahead to kill.
Oh, midnight come and end today
Though I do not wish to sit
Alone another midnight in the dark

Tonight I write

I love to hear the words you write:
They lift me and excite
With visions of another world
That should be ours.

"A bird with backward bending knees
Struts on the shoreline by the trees
As tide remakes a river;
"A heron on a Cornish beach."

"Salt water's creeping
Into Cornish creeks,
Flooding into Cornish coves."

"I think of these as I sit alone
Up here on Primrose Hill
And hear a drone
Of bombers not our own"

"While in the vale"
The bomb-lit fires grow
And a city's burning long ago."

"This is what I write
In the dark recesses of the night:
I write of sadness and the lack of you."
"But in my selfish greed
For you I let you down
For you are weaker than you pretend
And need the strength of two."

October Rain and Laughter

"An October day of rain and laughter;
Will air again be ever dry?
Wind itself is wholly water,
Water and your laughter."

"Where is the poetry and the laughter
In a life lived for mortar and for gain?
On an October day of rain and laughter
We share our passion and our pain."

Rain in October

Trees are October green and brown
And ocean rain is teeming down.

You phoned today. You always do
When I allow. I heard your voice
And wanted you as I am wanting
You right now. A wild and fitful night.
A storm is bending each wet bough.

Most men, I think, are merely takers,
Driven by a need to use and own,
But you are a giver and the given
And yet you have to live alone
Because all you want is me.

Trust

You are all I need to love
Me all my life and in return
I love you oh, so much.
How could I cope
Without the love I feel
In the rightness of your touch?

And yet I worry, fret, and grieve
That you might cool to me,
And leave. And yet I know

You as I know myself.
I see you in my soul and know
That we are one and I can know
None better underneath that shining sun.

No, I know you are unlike the rest.
I *know*. I do not have to trust.

Somewhere in your Mind

"Somewhere, somewhere
In your mind is fear
That I may not be
What I appear.
Yet too much pain
And hurt I've seen
To be unkind."

"I see the end of life
And know that only love
Can carry us to Love."

"To be unkind is to be
Undone. To be undone
Is die in shame and lose
Forever salvation
And your name."

"I am too old to be unkind.
You are my passageway
To Heaven through the love
I have for you."

"In your hurt you hurt me
And what lotion do I have
But love to soothe your pain?
It is all the ointment
That I have to cure your cares
And therefore mine."

"No, in me is nothing that's unkind:
The fear is only in your mind.
A hurt-bred fear. I am exactly as I appear."

By a City Pond

"Today again we failed to meet.
I spent my time in Camley Street
In that little patch of ponds and trees
Between the railroad and the waterway,"

"In the rustle of the reeds
And ash trees only half as old as me;
Ashes to ashes, trees to dust,
If you Love don't get you
Then the Devil must
For Love when lost is lust
And Lust is sin
That lets the cloven Devil in."

October on the Hill

October's ruin is on the hill
And November's ruin marks us too
In smaller and in bigger ways
With the dying of our shorter days
And the dying of the long decades.

The dying sun's distress
Distresses too the dying trees
And never again will there ever be
This year's sunlight on the sea.

Despair

"I have not learned to ride your mood
Or let it pass. I respond in fear
As though that mood will always last.
But a mood with you is such
A passing thing I should let it go,
Accept its sting, and comfort you."

"But I hear the tolling of the passing bell
Telling us of the lateness of our lives;
Telling us we are the unliving
Dying in a house of ruin in the rain."

Part Two

Island in the Tide

There is a hill of stone
And soil upon the sand
And tide will make an island
Of that land. Love, unmake and isle
Of me and leave me not abandoned
To the sea.

Hedgehog

A fox, they say, knows many things;
But I am prickles in a ball,

For in one lone thought I carry all:
Love is the creator and what is made.

What other knowledge can there be?
Mere wavelets on a deep blue sea.

Maker and the Made

There is no knower,
Only what is known;
Thought without a thinker
(Thought there is alone)
But thought when stilled is love

And unmattered thought
Above the brain
Also stills to love again.

Love is then the maker
And the made
And all that we can know.

Master?

Are you my Master?
Can Love be Lord?

Can Love create the war-plane,
The ploughshare and the sword?
Yes, for I make a claim to know.

Love makes the wild swans fly,
Love makes life,
So what can make you die?

Loss

Continuity has all but gone
Like the setting of a sun
For we've been taken in
By the folly of the Jacobin.

But the loss of love
Is the loss that kills,
Love that made the sea
And laid the rising hills.

Li Po

Quietly I am sitting down
In a Chinese tea shop in Camden Town,
Amid the semi-singing tones of Mandarin
And March in eastern cold is setting in.

Reaching into a river for the moon
Long ago Li Po the poet drowned.
Ignoring the nature of how things are
Will never get you very far
And in the end will bring you down.

Li Po the poet believed that sin
Is disobeying the law within,
That fire must burn, and the burn
Must drown.

We, in turn, believe that sin
Is ignoring the love that lies within;
Within, above, beneath, below
Even the poet, the great Li Po,
And his fine unbottled wine.

Englisc

Summer never seems to shine
So a priest has broken Woden's shrine:

From bletsian to bless,
From bled and bleed to bliss?
Love is God and Love is all there is.

Love-Lies-Bleeding

Love-lies-bleeding is a flower:
But can love bleed? Life lies
Bleeding when love we lack
For love we always need.

Yet I marvel at the human race,
Those who lack the grace of love
Yet strive so hard to stay alive:
Something, I think, I never did.

Photograph, Burma, 1944

A lean lance-jack, a milkman-
Muleteer, smiles in youth
Across the years. Ladling milk

From door to door, he'd never
Heard of the Service Corps.

Corporal, out of Burma did you come,
Survive beyond Millennium?

The long battalions march away
From Rangoon and Mandalay.

So many men then fought and died
And still the world's uncivilised.

Time

Rocks erode and ride,
Rising as they go like clouds,
But aeons, aeons slow.

A pterodactyl's gliding on hot hide
By a bare hillside
And a coelocanthèd sea.

Downs laid down to lie
In a sun-bright sea.
No Roman yet had come to Rye,
No keel is over Pevensey.

No men then,
No men there'll be again:
But Love is always there

Change and the Changeless

In this grate is a fire of ferns:
After sixty million years a forest burns.

And once I stood on Beachy Head,
Stood on the bodies of the dead,
Dead sea-things now high in air.

For all things change, we're told,
And we are forever growing old
And coccoliths, now wet with rain,
Once were fathoms deep and south of Spain.
But what remains the same is love.

Dido

Lightning lit the spider's web
And thus was widow Dido wed,
Before she died from loss of love.

But who freed Dido into Dis?
Love can do much more than this.

Icarus

We are therefore unafraid
Since Love is the maker and the made
And the lover and the loved can never die.

Love soars above all other things:
It is no Icarus with brief wax wings.

The Holy Grail

What comfort can we bring
To a groin-gone Fisher-King?

But I at last now know for sure
For a crippled king there is a cure:
There is no Wasteland where there's love.

The Odyssey in Brief

Why leave a morning world
For a world of mourning;
Immortal life for war
And mortal wife and dung
And dying dogs on a rock
Too short for horses?

Because human love is all there is:
It is all our truth and all our bliss:
And we can know no more than this.